CONTENTS

Bloopers, scripture, quote, repeat

Thank you

We had a lot of young couples with babies visiting our growing church, so mom wanted to let them know we had a nursery for their convenience. She wrote in the bulletin:

We are so glad you are here! If you have children and don't know it, we have a nursery.

(Do people have kids they forgot about?)

God is good, Brother Bill is better!

God assumed from the beginning that the wise of the world would view Christians as fools... and He has not been disappointed... If I have brought any message today, it is this:

Have the courage to have your wisdom regarded as stupidity.

Be fools for Christ.

And have the courage to suffer the contempt of the sophisticated world.

~ Justice Antonin Scalia

A merry heart makes a cheerful countenance,

But by sorrow of the heart the spirit is broken.

Proverbs 15:13 NKJV

The fear of the Lord is the beginning of knowledge, but fools despise wisdom and instruction.

Proverbs 1:7 NKJV

<u>*Mom's Church bulletin Bloopers*</u>

Reba and Don request your presents at their wedding Friday night.

(Come if you can, just be sure to send those presents!)

We needed a Sunday School teacher another week, so mom wrote:

Please pray as we still need a 4-5 year old Sunday School teacher.

(We start our kids teaching early!)

To me, the best way to witness is to not spend all your time explaining to them how wrong they are on everything they are doing, but to show them how your life is working and how much peace you have.

Jesus was never the least bit judgmental.

~ Brad Paisley

And we know that ALL things

work together for GOOD

to those who LOVE GOD,

to those who are the called

according to HIS purpose.

Romans 8:28 NKJV

<u>Mom's Church bulletin Bloopers</u>

Mom was announcing the upcoming Bible school and some of the fun activities that would be going on. Listed were:

"relay races, arts and crafts and TURDLE races."

(Poor mom turned scarlet when the spelling error was brought to her attention.)

God can use anything and anyone for good, even snakes!   ~

Never have more children than you have car windows.

~ Erma Bombeck

*Cleanliness becomes more important when godliness is
unlikely.   ~ P.J. O'Rourke*

Funny thing is the poorer people are, the more generous they seem to be.

~ Dolly Parton

*For I have given REST
to the weary and
JOY to the sorrowing.*
Jeremiah 31:25 NLT

*For I have satiated the weary soul,
and I have replenished every sorrowful soul.*
Jeremiah 31:25 KJV

<u>Mom's Church bulletin Bloopers</u>

Our choir Director would like to invite anyone who enjoys sinning, to join our choir.

(Sounds like a fun choir! I got some mileage out of that one!)

A worm welcome to all our visitors today!

In the Christmas program:

They brought gifts of gold, Frankenstein and myrrh.

There has NEVER been a time when God didn't direct, protect, or correct me.

There may have been times where I was less than faithful to Him, but He had FAITH IN ME.

~ Denzel Washington

To be a peacemaker, you must know the Peace giver.

~ Rev. Billy Graham

A person's WISDOM yields PATIENCE;

it is to one's glory to overlook an offense.

Proverbs 19:11 NIV

The discretion of a man makes him SLOW TO ANGER,

And his glory is to overlook a transgression.

Proverbs 19:11 NKJV

Church bulletin Bloopers

The Associate pastor revealed the churches new tithing campaign slogan last week. "I upped My Pledge ----Up Yours."

"Remember in prayer the many who are sick of our congregation."

"We pray that our people will jumble themselves..."

One of the things I pray for on a daily basis is that whatever God wants me to be doing, it's reflected through my actions, how I deal with other people, the way I do my job.

And I hope I do it in a way that pleases Him.

~ Alton Brown

Food Network Host

The one who is IN YOU

is GREATER

than the one who is in the world.

1 John 4:4b NIV

Dear friends, let us LOVE ONE ANOTHER,

for love comes from God.

1 John 4:7a NIV

<u>*Church bulletin Bloopers*</u>

We need more volunteers to spit up groceries for our food baskets.

Albert, John and Mary's oldest sin, will be graduating this year.

Come back next week! Our pastor will be gone so you can hear a good sermon by Brother Lowell.

To succeed in life you need three things; a wishbone, a backbone and a funny bone.

~ Reba McEntire

No man has a good enough memory to be a successful liar.

~ Abraham Lincoln

Try to define the trinity and you'll lose your mind. Deny it and you'll lose your soul.

~ Adrian Rogers

For God loved the world in this way:

He gave His one and

ONLY SON,

so that everyone who BELIEVES in Him will
not perish but have

ETERNAL LIFE.

John 3:16 CSB

<u>*Church bulletin Bloopers*</u>

Don't let worry kill you off –

Let the church help!

During the absence of our pastor, we had the rare privilege of hearing a good sermon by Brother Ayers.

Sister Barbara is still in the hospital and is having trouble sleeping. She requests CD's of our pastor's sermons.

Most people don't want to give up their ego. Someone told me a long time ago that EGO means to ETCH GOD OUT, without God, one is not that strong. He sees us.

~ Jim Caviezel

Jesus is the inspiration for anyone to go the distance.

~ Sylvester Stallone

It's impossible to hold up the banners of victim and victory at the same time.
~ Lysa Terkeurst

For I am persuaded that neither death nor life, nor angels nor principalities nor powers, nor things present nor things to come, nor height nor depth, nor any other created thing, shall be able to separate us from the love of God which is in Christ Jesus our Lord.

Romans 8:38-39 NKJV

<u>Church bulletin Bloopers</u>

Mary Smith has volunteered to strip and refinish the communion table in the sanctuary.

Our spring revival will be hell May 14-19.

The pastor would appreciate it if the ladies of our congregation would lend him their electric girdles for the pancake breakfast next Sunday morning.

I'M A CHRISTIAN.
…In Chariots of Fire, the runner Eric Liddell says, "When I run, I feel His pleasure." And I feel that pleasure when I act and it's going well, particularly on-stage…Before I go onstage every night, I pause and dedicate the performance to GOD, in the sense of "ALLOW ME TO SURRENDER."

~ Hugh Jackman

The steadfast love of the Lord never ceases;
*HIS **MERCIES NEVER** COME TO AN **END**.*
Lamentations 3:22 ESV

Through the Lord's mercies we are not
consumed,
Because HIS COMPASSIONS FAIL NOT.
Lamentations 3:22 NKJV

A mother was teaching her 3-year-old daughter the Lord's prayer.

Every night she would repeat it after her mother. One night she was ready to "do it myself" so the mother beamed with pride and listened as her daughter recited perfectly till the end when she said,

"Lead us not into temptation but deliver us some e-mail. Amen"

There is no promise God cannot keep, No prayer God will not answer, And NO PROBLEM TOO HARD FOR HIM TO SOLVE.

~ Adrian Rogers

I think you'd be foolish NOT to believe in God.

~ Tom Hanks

At the end of the day, the enemy is going to be sorry he ever messed with you.

~ Priscilla Shirer

COME to me all of you who are

TIRED from the heavy burden you have been
forced to carry.

I will GIVE you REST.

Matthew 11:28 ERV

COME UNTO ME,

all ye that labour and

are heavy laden,

and I will give you REST.

Matthew 11:28 KJV

A funeral parlor hired a new Assistant to make the memorial programs. On the front of the flier he wrote:

Remember that you are butt dust and into dust you shall return.

A child in Sunday school was so proud to tell what she remembered from the lesson I taught:

"All men have sinned, and God is short."

When you feel overwhelmed and you're tempted to take everything into your own hands, you have to make yourself be still. The battle is not yours. The battle is the Lord's.

~ Joel Osteen

Is prayer your steering wheel or your spare tire?

~ Corrie Ten Boom

I leave you PEACE.
It is my own peace I give you.
I give you peace in a different way than the world does.
John 14:27a ERV

Peace I leave with you,
MY PEACE
I GIVE TO YOU;
not as the world gives do I give you…   *John 14:27 NKJV*

My nephew to my niece: "which hurts worse? When I do this," (he hits her with edge of plastic sword) "or when I do this?" (hits her with the flat side of the plastic sword.) Brothers!

Two elderly gentlemen sat outside the nursing home on a bench. "I'm 84 years old and everything I have aches and barely works. You're about my age, how do you feel?"

"I feel like a newborn baby" replied the second gentleman. "Really? You feel like a newborn baby?!"

"Absolutely! No hair, no teeth, and I think I just wet my pants."

Everyone can relate to love, hurt, pain, learning how to forgive, need to get over, needing the power of God in their life.

~ Tyler Perry

The only one who won't fail you is the one I put my trust in. That'd be Jesus, the Son of God.

~ Si Robertson

Duck Dynasty

For All have sinned and fall short of the glory of God.

Romans 3:23 NKJV

*But God shows His love for us in that **while we were still sinners,** Christ died for us.*

Romans 5:8 ESV

My husband told me:

Roses are red

And other colors too.

I don't really like flowers,

But I sure love you!

What is green and smells like paint?

Green paint

I FOUND GOD DOING "FURY."

I became a Christian man…in a very real way. I could have just said the prayers that were on the page. But it was a real thing that really saved me.

~ Shia LaBeouf

You can't defeat the demons you enjoy playing with.

~ Author unknown

You don't need a plan; you just need to be present. ~Bob Goff

Yet in all these things we are

MORE than conquerors

THROUGH HIM

who loved us.

Romans 8:37 NKJV

No, despite all these things,

OVERWHELMING

VICTORY

IS OURS

THROUGH

CHRIST,

who loved us.

Romans 8:37 NLT

Our then, 4-year-old granddaughter, wraps her tiny arms around Grandpa's neck and says, "I love you Grandpa!"

You can almost see him melting until she continues, "But not as much as I love Grammy!"

My husband Bob tells me he's going to buy a little robot dog and put a watch inside him. Then he's going to take the dog to the vet and have him checked for ticks.

Why do they call it rush hour when nothing moves?

~ Robin Williams

Electricity is really just organized lightning.

~ George Carlin

They say marriages are made in heaven. But so is thunder and lightning.

~Clint Eastwood

Are not two sparrows sold for a penny? And not one of them will fall to the ground apart from your Father.

But even the hairs of your head are all numbered.

Fear not, therefore; you are of more value than many sparrows.

Matthew 10:29-31 ESV

When my grandson asked me how old I was, I teasingly replied, "I'm not sure…"

"Look in your underwear, Grammy," he advised, "mine says I'm 4 to 5."

Girl: Why would someone dress like a hamster?

Mom: You mean a hipster?

Girl: What's the difference?

I pray to be a good servant to God, a father, a husband, a brother and uncle, a good neighbor, a good leader to those who look up to me and a good follower to those that are serving God and doing the right thing.

~ Mark Wahlberg

I've read the last page of the Bible, it's all going to turn out all right.

~ Rev. Billy Graham

"So remember that the Lord your God is the ONLY God, and you can trust Him!

He keeps His agreement. He shows His love and kindness to all people who love Him and obey his commands.

He continues to show his love and kindness through a thousand generations,"

Deuteronomy 7:9 ERV

My mom, who has dementia heard: Fun to be a puppy and a ninja turtle too!

They actually said: If you want to be as happy as the woman in the shoe...

My husband Bob told me: "when we renew our vowels, I'll take A and E, you can have IOU."

I pray that you all put your shoes way under the bed at night so that you gotta get on your knees in the morning to find them, and while you're down there thank God for grace and mercy and understanding.

~ Denzel Washington

Faith goes up the stairs that love has built and looks out the windows which hope has opened.

~ Charles Spurgeon

Start where you are. Use what you have. Do what you can.   *~ Arthur Ashe*

Do not be anxious about anything, but in every situation, by prayer and petition, with thanksgiving, present your requests to God. And the peace of God which transcends all understanding, will guard your hearts and your minds in Christ Jesus. *Philippians 4:6-7 NIV*

My husband Bob wants to be cremated and put in an urn. He wants a plaque on it that reads:

"Bob didn't earn his keep but I'm still keeping his urn."

Roses are red

Violets are blue

Everyone knows

I'm a sucker for you!

Mountaintops are for views and inspiration, but fruit is grown in the valleys.
~ Rev. Billy Graham

A feeling that I was doing what I was supposed to be doing – WHAT GOD GAVE ME THE TALENT TO DO. JOY….

It's that feeling you get when you really connect with the PURPOSE of your life.
~ Martina McBride

Then he said to them, "Go your way, eat the fat, drink the sweet, and send portions to those whom nothing is prepared; for this day is holy to our Lord.

DO NOT SORROW,

for the JOY of the Lord

is your STRENGTH."

Nehemiah 8:10 NKJV

I was trying to stay current on all the abbreviations the kids use today. I text my son who lives in North Carolina, and asked "When are you coming in?" He didn't answer for a while, so I typed "wtf?"

He immediately responded back: "Do you know what that means?!"

Me: "Wednesday, Thursday or Friday."

Him: "Not even close mom!"

After I released "Jesus take the Wheel", people started saying oh, it's kind of risky. You're coming out with a religious song.

And I was thinking, really? I grew up in Oklahoma, I always had a close relationship with God.

I never thought it was risky *in the least.*

If anything, I thought IT WAS THE SAFEST THING I COULD DO!

~ Carrie Underwood

CHRIST is the one

who GIVES me the

STRENGTH I need

to do whatever I must do.

Philippians 4:13 ERV

A married couple, both 60 years old, were celebrating their 35th anniversary. During their party, a fairy appeared to congratulate them and grant them each one wish.

The wife wanted to travel around the world. The fairy waved her wand and poof - the wife had tickets in her hand for a world cruise.

Next, the fairy asked the husband what he wanted.

He said; "I wish I had a wife 30 years younger than me."

So the fairy picked up her wand and poof - the husband was 90.

…People think God doesn't pay attention to the details. God is IN the details.

~ John Schneider

A true Christian, living an obedient life, is a constant rebuke to those who accept the moral standards of this world.

~ Rev. Billy Graham

WATCH therefore, for you do not know what hour your Lord is coming.
Matthew 24:42 NKJV

... CHOOSE this day whom you will serve...

But as for me and my house, we will serve the LORD.

Joshua 24:15 NKJV

Dementia is a terrible, incurable disease. It runs in our family. I trust God in the midst of caring for others who have it and try to find humor wherever I can.

Mom told me yesterday:

"I'm not gonna eat. They can be obnoxious cause they're black and white and it's snowing."

It was 85 degrees out, but I smiled and said "Ok, but I'll get you ice cream if you eat some food."

Problem solved. (Ice cream is her top comfort food.)

*The most important lesson we are supposed to be learning right now is how completely **lost** we are **without God.***

If we don't learn this lesson, then our lives are going to have zero meaning.

~ Brian "Head" Welch

Former Korn guitarist

Don't magnify your problems, MAGNIFY YOUR GOD…he's got you covered.

~Tony Evans

"In my Father's house are many mansions; if it were not so, I would have told you. I go to prepare a place for you.

And if I go and prepare a place for you,

I WILL COME AGAIN and receive you to myself; that where I am, there you may be also."

John 14:2-3 NKJV

Sister Mary was truly a religious woman. Besides for her duties as a nun, she was also very active in various hospitals visiting sick patients and taking care of all their needs.

It was no surprise that one day when she ran out of gas, the only container she could find to put the gas into was a bedpan.

Sister Mary happily walked two blocks to the closest gas station filled up the bedpan with gas and headed back to her car. Luck would have it that as Sister Mary started tipping the gas into the fuel tank, the traffic light turned red and she had quite a large audience witnessing the spectacle.

Just when she finished pouring in the last drops of gas a fellow opened his window and hollered, "I swear! If that car starts, I'm becoming a religious man!"

My HELP COMES

from the LORD, who made heaven and earth.

Psalms 121:2 NKJV

Restore to me the JOY

of your salvation, and uphold me by your generous spirit.

Psalms 51:12 NKJV

Santa saw your Facebook posts. This year you're getting a dictionary.

~ Anonymous

Sit down and let me tell you a story. Once upon a time I was hungry and that's what happened to all your chocolate.

~ Anonymous

Since there is only one of me, I'm obviously a limited edition!

I've been very guilty of not showing my faith and just praying when I needed it, when something bad happened in my life and not being thankful when things turned out good. All good is from God, and so I want to honor him.

~ Kevin James

The quickest way to double your money is to fold it over and put it back in your wallet.

~ Will Rogers

Let not your heart envy sinners,
but continue in the fear of the Lord all the day.

Proverbs 23:17 ESV

For the Son of Man will come in the glory of
His Father with His angels, and then He will
reward each according to his works.

Matthew 16:27 NKJV

I was a little surprised when my son suddenly announced one day after church, "I am thinking of being a Preacher when I grow up."

"Why is that?" I asked.

"Well, I figure I have to go to church on Sundays anyway, and I think it'll be more fun to stand and yell than to just sit and listen."

You are never too old to set another goal or to dream a new dream.   ~C.S. Lewis

The real opportunity for success lies within the person and not in the job.
~Zig Ziglar

Go to heaven for the climate, hell for the company.
~ Mark Twain

From there to here, and here to there, funny things are everywhere.
~ Dr. Seuss

Now may the God of hope fill you with all joy and peace in believing, that you may abound in hope by the power of the Holy Spirit.

Romans 15:13 ESV

Therefore, since we have been justified by faith, we have peace with God through our Lord Jesus Christ.

Romans 5:1 ESV

At my granddaughter's 12th birthday lunch a trivia game broke out.

The question: Who is the actor who played Burt in Mary Poppins?

My granddaughter: ummm… I know it …

it's Bernie Sanders!

What keys can't open locks?

Monkeys, donkeys and turkeys.

I AM A PROUD CHRISTIAN! Because of Christ's message of peace, love and forgiveness.

Those three things will save the world and I revere that.

~ Sean Astin

The constitution was never meant to prevent people from praying; it's declared purpose was to PROTECT THEIR FREEDOM TO PRAY.

~ Ronald Reagan

But let all those rejoice who put their trust in You;

Let them ever

SHOUT FOR JOY,

because You defend them;

Let those also who love Your name be JOYFUL IN YOU.

Psalm 5:11 NKJV

Everything is funny,

as long as it's happening

to somebody else.

~Will Rogers

If you're not hungry for God, you're probably full of yourself.

~ Author Unknown

When trouble comes, focus on GOD'S ABILITY to care for you.   ~ Charles Stanley

The devil knows your name but calls you by your sin. God knows your sin but calls you by your name.

~ Ricardo Sanchez

Don't concentrate on what you lack, concentrate on what you have. Then give all of it to Jesus for His use.

~ Anne Graham Lotz

Do not let your heart be troubled, nor let it be fearful .

John 14:27 b NASB

Do not let your hearts be troubled and DO NOT BE AFRAID.

John 14:27b NIV

Weeping may endure for a night,

But JOY comes in the morning.

Psalm 30:5

I can do ALL THINGS

THROUGH CHRIST

Who

STRENGTHENS ME.

Philippians 4:13 NKJV

Jesus not only kept Himself from engaging in evil,

He also continually acted in ways that honored and glorified God.

He not only continually avoided the negative, He always pursued the positive.

~ David Jeremiah

However softly we speak,

God is near enough to hear us.

~ St. Teresa of Avila

Harry walked over to the Priest after services, "You know Father, I am really stuck in a quandary I would like to attend church next week, but I just can't miss the big game next Sunday, it's just out of the question." "Oh Harry" said the Priest putting his arm around Harry, "don't you know? That's what recorders are for." Harry's face lit up "you mean I could record your sermon?"

~ Anonymous

Be anxious for nothing, but in everything by prayer and supplication, with thanksgiving, let your requests be made known to God; and the peace of God, which surpasses all understanding, will guard your hearts and minds through Christ Jesus.

Philippians 4:6-7 NKJV

The Bible tells us that Jesus Christ came to do three things.

He came to have my

past FORGIVEN,

you get a PURPOSE for living

and a HOME in Heaven.

~ Rick Warren

Feed your fears and your faith will starve. Feed your faith, and your fears will.

~ Max Lucado

The truth is like a lion. You don't have to defend it. Let it loose. It will defend itself.

~ St. Augustine

As for me – let's be clear – no riding the fence here – my absolute belief is in a LOVING and ALL KNOWING and POWERFUL GOD and the teachings of JESUS CHRIST.

~ Corbin Bernsen

For the wages of sin is death, but the gift of God is eternal life in Christ Jesus our Lord.

Romans 6:23 NKJV

Jesus said to him, "I am the way, the truth, and the life. No one comes to the Father

EXCEPT THROUGH ME."

John 14:6 NKJV

Repent therefore and be converted, that your sins may be blotted out, so that times of refreshing may come from the presence of the Lord,

Acts 3:19 NKJV

The Lord is near to ALL who call upon Him, to all who call upon Him in truth.

Psalms 145:18 NKJV

For "Everyone who calls on the name of the Lord

WILL BE SAVED"

Romans 10:13 ESV

For with the HEART one believes and is justified, and with the MOUTH one confesses and is saved.

Romans 10:10 ESV

When I struggle with forgiveness, I think of how God forgave me by not holding the past against me.

Then I can't help but FORGIVE.

Never be too stubborn to say "I'm sorry."

~ Jessica Robertson

Duck Dynasty

God doesn't require us to succeed, he only requires that you TRY.

~ Mother Teresa

Religious life is an encounter with the living God.

Sometimes that encounter is preceded by a kind of soul -searching agony that tries desperately not to hear, runs in the opposite direction, and frantically tries to reason itself out of answering the invitation.

~ Mother Angelica

Worry does not empty tomorrow of its sorrow, it empties today of its strength.   ~ Corrie Ten Boom

And I am convinced that **nothing can ever separate us from God's love.** *Neither death nor life, neither angels or demons, neither our fears for today nor our worries about tomorrow –* **not even the powers of hell can separate us from God's love.**

No power in the sky above or in the earth below – indeed, nothing in all creation will ever be able to separate us from the love of God that is revealed in Christ Jesus our Lord.

Romans: 38-39 NLT

I will

NEVER LEAVE YOU
nor forsake you.

Hebrews 13:5b

A merry heart does good, like medicine, but a broken spirit dries the bones.

Proverbs 17:22 NKJV

When I stand before God at the end of my life, I would hope that I would not have a single bit of talent left and could say, I used everything you gave me.

~ Erma Bombeck

I make no apologies for the fact that I have a religious life of my own. I'm speaking as a Christian because I'm speaking as myself.

~ Krista Tippett

Never wrestle with a pig. You'll both get dirty and the pig likes it!

~ Anonymous

Don't worry about what to wear today. Your smile goes with every outfit.

~ Anonymous

Never let your best friends get lonely….keep bugging them.   *~ Anonymous*

The Lord is on my side;

I will NOT FEAR.

What can man do to me?

Psalms 118:6 ESV

Do not be wise in your own eyes; Fear the Lord and depart from evil.

Proverbs 3:7 NKJV

How does a train eat?

Chew, chew

You never know when a moment and a few sincere words can have an impact on a life.

~ Zig Ziglar

If you only knock long enough and loud enough at the gate, you are sure to wake somebody up.

~ Henry Longfellow

By perseverance the snail reached the Ark.

~ Charles Spurgeon

Happiness is a perfume you cannot pour on others without getting a few drops on yourself.

~ Ralph Waldo Emmerson

Duct tape is like the force. It has a light side, a dark side, and it holds the world together.

~Paul Fix

ASK, and it will be given to you.

SEEK, and you will find.

KNOCK, and the door will be opened to you.

Matthew 7:7 CSB

People with goals succeed because they know where they are going… It's as simple as that.

~ Earl Nightingale

A good plan today is better than a great plan tomorrow.

~ General George S. Patton

Nothing is particularly hard if you divide it into small jobs.

~ Henry Ford

What the mind can conceive and believe, it can achieve.

~ Napoleon Hill

I long to accomplish a great and noble task, but it is my chief duty to accomplish small tasks as if they were great and noble.

~ Hellen Keller

*TRUST in the Lord
with ALL YOUR HEART,
and lean not on your own understanding; in
all your ways acknowledge Him,
and He shall direct your paths.*

Proverbs 3:5-6 NKJV

*His love for His followers is as high above us
as heaven is above the earth.*

Psalms 103:11 ERV

I am content to fill a little space if God be glorified.

~Susanna Wesley

I'm a Christian now…I go surfing and snow-boarding and I'm always around nature. I look at everything and think:

"WHO COULDN'T BELIEVE THERE'S A GOD?

Is all this a mistake?" It just blows me away.

~ Paul Walker

The world today doesn't make sense, so why should I paint pictures that do?

~ Pablo Picasso

Faith and fear don't co-exist.

You live in one or the other.

Choose Faith.

*For He shall give His angels charge over you
to keep you in all your
ways.*   *Psalms 91:11* NKJV

*People judge by what is on the outside, but the
Lord looks at the
heart.*   *1 Samuel 16:7b* ERV

For we live by FAITH,

NOT BY SIGHT.

2 Corinthians 5:7 NIV

In my father's house are many mansions; if it were not so, I would have told you. I go to prepare a place for you.

And if I go to prepare a place for you,

I WILL COME AGAIN

and receive you to myself; that where I am,

there you may be also.

John 14:2-3 NKJV

As iron sharpens iron, so one person sharpens another.

Proverbs 27:17 NIV

A glad heart makes a cheerful face, but by sorrow of the heart the spirit is crushed.

Proverbs 15:13 ESV